Rookie National Parks™

Glacier National Park

by Joanne Mattern

Content Consultant
National Park Service

Reading Consultant
Jeanne M. Clidas, Ph.D.
Reading Specialist

Children's Press®
An Imprint of Scholastic Inc.

Library of Congress Cataloging-in-Publication Data
Names: Mattern, Joanne, 1963- author.
Title: Glacier National Park/by Joanne Mattern.
Description: New York, NY: Children's Press, an imprint of Scholastic Inc.,
2018. | Series: Rookie national parks | Includes bibliographical references and
index.
Identifiers: LCCN 2017023158| ISBN 9780531231944 (library binding: alk.
paper) | ISBN 9780531230930 (pbk.: alk. paper)
Subjects: LCSH: Glacier National Park (Mont.)—Juvenile literature.
Classification: LCC F737.G5 M38 2018 | DDC 978.6/52—dc23
LC record available at https://lccn.loc.gov/2017023158

Produced by Spooky Cheetah Press
Design: Judith Christ-Lafond/Ed LoPresti Graphic Design

© 2018 by Scholastic Inc. All rights reserved.

Published in 2018 by Children's Press, an imprint of Scholastic Inc.

Printed in Heshan, China 62

SCHOLASTIC, CHILDREN'S PRESS™, ROOKIE NATIONAL PARKS™, and
associated logos are trademarks and/or registered trademarks of Scholastic Inc.

1 2 3 4 5 6 7 8 9 10 R 27 26 25 24 23 22 21 20 19 18

Scholastic, Inc., 557 Broadway, New York, NY 10012

Table of Contents

Introduction **5**

1. Mighty Mountains **9**

2. Water and Ice **13**

3. Wild Places **17**

4. Stunning Sights **23**

Field Guide **26**

Where Is Ranger Red Fox? **28**

Leaf Tracker **30**

Glossary **31**

Index **32**

Facts for Now **32**

About the Author **32**

Welcome to Glacier National Park!

Glacier is in Montana. It was made a **national park** in 1910. People visit national parks to explore nature.

There are many incredible things to see in this park. There are **glaciers**, of course! There are also big mountains and beautiful waterfalls.

United States

←**Montana**

Glacier
National Park

N
W—◯—E
S

A big mountain **ridge** runs through Glacier. It cuts the park into different parts. Because of the split, the park has two separate climates. Some parts are warm and wet. Others are very cold and dry.

Glacier National Park borders a park in Canada. Together they are called an International Peace Park.

Chief Mountain was one of the first mountains to appear on a map of the area.

Chief Mountain can be seen from 100 miles (161 kilometers) away!

Chapter 1

Mighty Mountains

There are 175 mountains in Glacier National Park. One is Chief Mountain. It is more than 9,000 feet (2,743 meters) tall. That is more than six times as tall as the Empire State Building! People enjoy hiking on this big mountain.

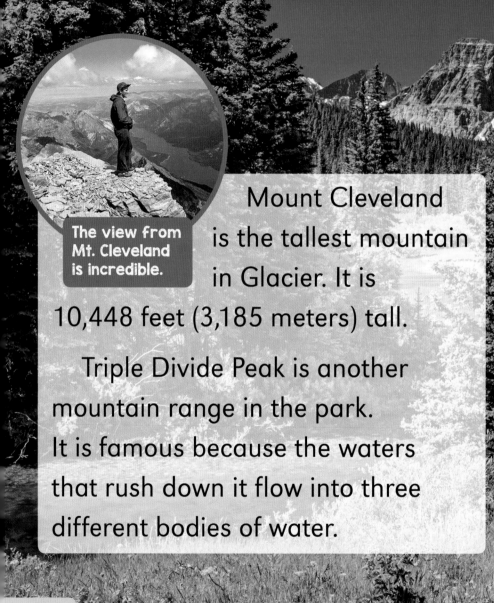

The view from Mt. Cleveland is incredible.

Mount Cleveland is the tallest mountain in Glacier. It is 10,448 feet (3,185 meters) tall.

Triple Divide Peak is another mountain range in the park. It is famous because the waters that rush down it flow into three different bodies of water.

There are more than 700 miles (1,127 kilometers) of hiking trails in Glacier.

Blackfoot Glacier is named for the Blackfeet Indians who live in the area.

This Blackfoot woman is wearing traditional clothing. She is competing in a fancy-dance competition.

Chapter 2

Water and Ice

There are 26 glaciers in this park. These large, thick blocks of ice are about 7,000 years old. Two of the largest are Harrison Glacier and Blackfoot Glacier. Like all of the glaciers in the park, though, they are getting smaller every year.

A grizzly bear can be up to 8 feet (2.4 meters) tall!

A mountain goat's thick coat helps it stay warm in winter.

Chapter 3

Wild Places

Glacier is home to a variety of **ecosystems**. Many different animals live in these areas.

Grizzly bears, black bears, and wolves can be found in the forests. Elk and deer graze in the grassy fields. And mountain goats roam over Glacier's rocky ridges.

Many smaller animals and birds live in the park, too. Marmots, beavers, and foxes live in the forests and prairies.

Wolves can go two weeks without food.

Some birds, like the ptarmigan (**tar**-muh-guhn), live on the ground. Others, like the golden eagle, fly high above the park.

The ptarmigan's feathers turn white in winter.

Marmots are members of the squirrel family.

Glacier is too cold for most reptiles. Only the western painted turtle and two types of garter snake live here.

Cedar trees can grow taller than many buildings.

Huckleberries are a main food source for the park's grizzly bears.

Many different trees and flowers grow in Glacier. The western part of the park has many cedar forests. These big trees can be up to 6 feet (1.8 meters) wide. That is as wide as a grown-up is tall! The cedars block out the sun, so only moss and ferns grow on the forest floor.

In summer, wildflowers cover the ground.

Sweet huckleberries grow in the park.

Brave hikers can cross a cable bridge like this one.

Tour buses take visitors through the park.

Chapter 4

Stunning Sights

Many visitors to Glacier drive on Going-to-the-Sun Road. It crosses the middle of the park and passes near all the best sights in Glacier.

In addition to natural wonders, visitors can also see historical buildings as they travel within the park.

Imagine you could visit Glacier. What would you do there?

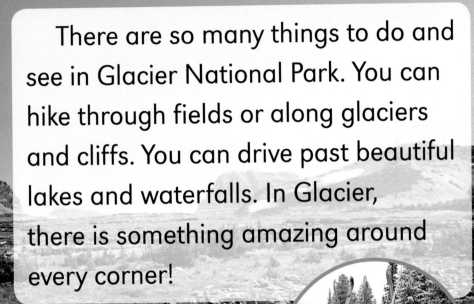

There are so many things to do and see in Glacier National Park. You can hike through fields or along glaciers and cliffs. You can drive past beautiful lakes and waterfalls. In Glacier, there is something amazing around every corner!

Cross-country skiing is a great way to explore Glacier in winter.

These are just some of the incredible animals that make their home in Glacier.

golden eagle

northern pike

willow ptarmigan

bighorn sheep

great horned owl

black bear

Wildlife by the Numbers

The park is home to about...

276 types of birds   **71** types of mammals

Mountain goats are the symbol of Glacier National Park.

elk

red fox

garter snake

mountain goat

grizzly bear

marmot

q types of reptiles and amphibians

24 types of fish

Oh no! Ranger Red Fox has lost his way in the park. But you can help. Use the map and the clues below to find him.

1. Ranger Red Fox started with a swim in the southwest part of Lake McDonald.

2. Then he walked northeast along Going-to-the-Sun Road.

3. Next, he walked through the woods to Grinnell Glacier.

4. Finally, he decided to head south to see about having a picnic with friends.

Help! Can you find me?

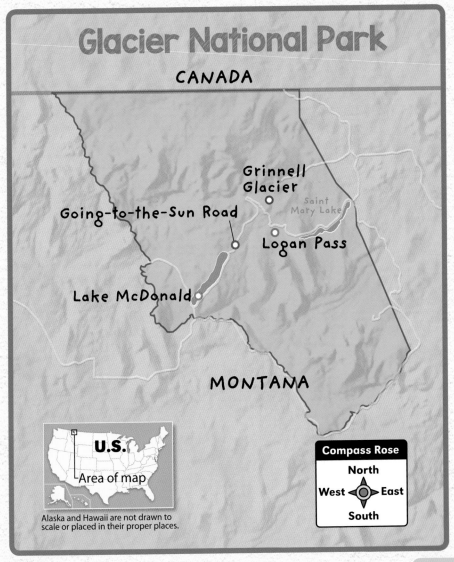

Glacier National Park

CANADA

Grinnell
Glacier

Saint
Mary Lake

Going-to-the-Sun Road

Logan Pass

Lake McDonald

MONTANA

U.S.

Area of map

Alaska and Hawaii are not drawn to
scale or placed in their proper places.

Compass Rose

North

West ◆ East

South

Can you guess which leaf belongs to which tree in Glacier? Read the clues to help you.

A.

1. Whitebark pine
Clue: This tree has long, sharp needles instead of leaves.

B.

2. Rocky Mountain maple
Clue: This tree's green leaves turn bright colors in fall.

3. Red cedar
Clue: The leaves of this tree are flat and feathery.

4. Aspen
Clue: This tree's leaves are round at the bottom and pointed at the top.

C.

D.

Answers: 1. C; 2. D; 3. A; 4. B

Glossary

ecosystems (**ee**-koh-sis-tuhms): all the living things in a place

glaciers (**glay**-shurz): huge blocks of slow-moving ice

national park (**nash**-uh-nuhl pahrk): area where the land and its animals are protected by the U.S. government

ridge (rij): long, narrow chain of mountains or hills

Index

animals 17–19, 20
Beaver Chief Falls 14
Blackfoot Glacier 12, 13
buildings 23
Chief Mountain 8, 9
climates 6
flowers 21
glaciers 5, 12, 13, 25

hiking 9, 11, 25
Going-to-the-Sun
Road 23
Harrison Glacier 13
International
Peace Park 7
Lake McDonald 14
lakes 14, 15, 25

Mount Cleveland 10
mountains 5, 6, 8,
9–10
Swiftcurrent Falls 14, 15
Swiftcurrent Lake 15
trees 21
Triple Divide Peak 10
waterfalls 5, 14, 15, 25

Facts for Now

Visit this Scholastic Web site for more information
on Glacier National Park:
www.factsfornow.scholastic.com
Enter the keyword Glacier

About the Author

Joanne Mattern has written more than 250 books for children.
She likes writing about natural wonders because she loves to
learn about the amazing places on our planet and the animals
and plants that live there. Joanne grew up in New York State and
still lives there with her husband, four children, and several pets.